Building
BARBECUES

FRANK GARDNER

MINI · WORKBOOK · SERIES

MURDOCH
B O O K S

CONTENTS

Barbecue with two fires (top left) and pit barbecue (bottom left)

Types of barbecue

There are many different types of barbecue and several different types of fuel. Before you start building a barbecue, consider which types will best suit your home and lifestyle.

CHOOSING A BARBECUE

A built barbecue can become a feature in the garden landscape and an integral part of your outdoor lifestyle. It will, however, require considerable time and effort spent on construction, so be sure you will use it often enough to justify your work. You don't want to create a 'white elephant' that is never used. In some cases a portable or mobile unit may suit your lifestyle better.

Here are some points to consider:
• For any barbecue you will need a level site, preferably one close to the house, but for a built barbecue it will have to be large enough for the structure and for the cook and helpers to move safely around it.
• The area where you entertain may not be suited to a built barbecue (it may be a deck or tiled patio), and so you may have to settle for a portable or mobile unit.
• You will need to have time and basic bricklaying or stoneworking skills to build the barbecue, or be prepared to pay someone to do it.
• If you usually barbecue for only a couple of people, it may be a waste of fuel to use a large, built structure.
• Likewise, if you have many of your barbecues away from home (on

picnics or holidays) you may find a portable barbecue more useful.
• You will probably find the cost of a built barbecue is similar to that of an equivalent mobile type.

BUILT BARBECUES

Built barbecues can be constructed for use with solid fuel or with a drop-in gas cooktop similar to those used in mobile barbecues. If you have plenty of wood on hand, fuel costs are nil. The costs of building a barbecue increase in proportion to the size and detail of the construction as well as with the choice of fuel.

PORTABLE AND MOBILE UNITS

Portable barbecues (those that can be packed up and put away or taken on picnics) and mobile barbecues (trolley types that can be moved to suit the weather or for storage) have become increasingly popular. They include electric barbecues, hibachi and kamado units, and kettle barbecues. However, these portable units are not very efficient when you are entertaining a large crowd and they often need to be stored or protected from the elements. They vary from simple types to elaborate

A built barbecue has the advantage that you can incorporate any number or size of preparation areas to suit your style of cooking and entertaining.

structures incorporating hoods, thermostats and side burners.

FUEL TYPES

Barbecues can be fired by a number of fuels. Those commonly used are solid fuels – such as wood, charcoal or briquettes – or gas or electricity.

SOLID FUELS

Solid fuels produce smoke, flames and smells that help create an 'outdoor' atmosphere. For some this is the essence of true barbecuing.

• Many people enjoy wood-fired barbecues for their traditional appeal,

but you need time to collect the wood and kindling and get the fire going: wood is not a fuel for the cook in a hurry. Cooking is done over hot coals, so patience is needed as the flames heat the hotplate and then subside to provide a stable plate temperature. Using firelighters, which are cubes of compressed kerosene, makes it easier to start a fire as they burn longer than paper. The smoke generated by wood-fired barbecues can be a problem, especially if the wind is changeable. If you live in a smoke control zone, there may be restrictions on open fires, so check with your local authority. But wood is cheap and if there is an adequate supply available a wood-fired barbecue will give years of maintenance-free enjoyment.

• Charcoal is the residue of partially burnt wood. It fires quickly and provides ample heat for the barbecue. Lighting is easy if small pyramids of charcoal are built over a firelighter. Once alight, the charcoal can be spread out. It gives off little smoke and adds to the aroma. Charcoal is available at hardware stores.

• Briquettes are basically compressed charcoal and tend to burn longer. They can be lit in the same manner as charcoal although some brands have been soaked in kerosene and are easier to light. However, they do not lose the kerosene smell after lighting.

GAS

Gas is a clean and efficient form of heat supply, enabling accurate temperature control at the turn of a knob. Plate temperature is reached quickly and can be controlled throughout the cooking process. If you have mains gas supplied for heating and cooking, you may be able to have a line and connection made for the barbecue, but this must be done by a licensed gasfitter. It is more common to use a gas bottle, which gives you greater freedom in siting the barbecue. Do ensure you have an adequate supply of bottled gas before you start cooking, as there's nothing worse than running out when you are halfway through.

Reusable lava rocks (pieces of volcanic rock) are sometimes placed in a tray between the burner and the hotplate or grill to spread the heat.

ELECTRICITY

Like gas, electricity is clean, efficient and provides excellent temperature control. Electric barbecues for domestic use are, however, limited in size as plug-in household power supply has a maximum of 3000 watts. Electricity can, therefore, be used to fuel only small units.

SMOKING CHIPS

Smoking chips can be burnt with the barbecue to add flavour to the food being cooked. Popular flavours include hickory or mesquite.

Wood is the natural choice of fuel for this barbecue in a pit, which was inspired by traditional campfires.

ADAPTING A CONVENTIONAL BARBECUE TO GAS

If you have a barbecue designed for solid fuel such as wood but find it is no longer practical, you can convert the existing firebox to accommodate a gas unit.

INSTALLING GAS BURNERS BENEATH THE EXISTING HOTPLATE

1 Measure the width and depth of the firebox beneath the hotplate. Purchase a drop-in burner unit to fit. These units come in a frame with from two to five gas burners, each with its own control knob. The unit dimensions will vary with different makes, but the figures in the table below will act as a guide. You will also need to purchase a gas bottle, regulator and hose.

2 The recommended spacing between the burners and the hotplate is 75 mm. This ensures adequate flame contact and heating of the cooking area. There are various ways of supporting the burner framework so that it is at the correct height.

- Position bricks or concrete blocks at either side of the firebox and set the framework on them.
- Determine the correct height on the walls either side of the firebox and fix metal angle to the walls using expansion bolts.
- Position flat lintel or rods of steel at the correct height across the front and rear of the firebox.

INSTALLING A COMPLETE NEW UNIT

Mobile gas barbecue units can be purchased without the trolley and placed into the firebox area. Measure the width and depth of the existing firebox and purchase a unit to fit. Remember that a unit with a roasting hood will need adequate space at the rear of the firebox so the hood can open fully.

As the unit will be exposed to all weather conditions, select one that has been finished completely in vitreous enamel or stainless steel. If possible, choose a unit with a cover that will protect the plate when the barbecue is not in use.

TYPICAL DROP-IN UNITS*

No. of burners	Length required	Depth required
2	430 mm	490 mm
3	610 mm	490 mm
4	760 mm	490 mm
5	960 mm	490 mm

* Precise measurements will vary. Check before you purchase a unit.

Sandstone blocks are used to decorative effect for the corners of this elegant natural gas barbecue, while brick walls form the sides and a cross-wall to support the slab below the gas unit. Sandstone is also used for the top.

Designing a barbecue

A built barbecue becomes a permanent part of the garden. It is worthwhile spending time to plan it carefully so that you get the result you want.

FACTORS TO CONSIDER

If you have decided that a built barbecue will suit you best, you will now have to decide on a design. This will depend on how much space you have, the type of fuel, and whether you need preparation areas and storage for wood or gas bottles. You will also need to consider whether to include a chimney, either real or decorative, and any other structures such as seating, planter boxes, walls or pergolas. Finally, consider how much you can afford to spend.

MATERIALS

The materials that you choose for your barbecue will depend on the style of your home, the formality or informality of your garden design, your budget and, of course, the availability of the materials.

Brick barbecues are the most common because of their ease of construction and their ability to tie the house and garden landscape together. If the barbecue is sited close to the house and the house is brick, you will need to choose bricks that match it. If this is not necessary, you should select bricks that will be able to withstand the heat of the barbecue, particularly if it is wood-fired. Avoid the softer, calcium-silicate bricks and choose well-burnt, dry-pressed bricks if possible. Your local brick supplier will be able to advise you.

Stone barbecues are also popular in areas where York stone, limestone and sandstone can be easily purchased. York stone lends itself to a natural, rustic setting and is an ideal choice for wood-fired, informal designs. Choose carefully, however, as some stones such as limestone can 'explode' when subjected to great heat. Sandstone is a softer, more porous stone and allows for shaping and facing. This makes it a popular choice in more formal and traditional settings. It can be purchased in regular geometric shapes in either block or slab form. Sandstone is also available in split, irregular forms.

DIMENSIONS

The dimensions to be considered include not only the overall length, width and height of the unit, but also those of the surface areas that will be used for cooking and preparation. You will also need to consider the space required for the firebox or gas unit, and storage for wood, gas bottles and other accessories.

BRICK MEASUREMENTS★

Number of bricks	Length (mm)	Height (mm)
1	215	75
2	440	150
3	665	225
4	890	300
5	1125	375
6	1350	450
7	1575	525
8	1800	600
9	2025	675
10	2250	750
11	2475	825
12	2700	900
13	2925	975
14	3150	1050
15	3275	1125

★ Including allowance for 10 mm joints. To include half a brick, add 112 mm to the length.

If you are working in brick or cut stone, design the barbecue to suit full brick or block dimensions. This will make laying easier and you will avoid unnecessary cutting. Brick sizes vary quite considerably, but a standard brick size is 215 mm long x 100 mm wide x 65 mm high. The table above gives the numbers of bricks necessary to make up various lengths or heights. If your bricks are a different size, adjust the measurements to suit.

HOTPLATE

The size of the area required for cooking depends on the number of people to be fed. An average sized cooking plate of 930 x 600 mm caters for 12–15 people. If you usually cook for smaller numbers, reduce the plate size to 690 x 600 mm and then if you occasionally need extra space, you can bring out or hire a portable barbecue to supplement it.

When deciding on a plate size, ensure it will suit the brickwork dimensions. The two plate sizes given here will fit inside standard brickwork with a 10 mm gap all round for expansion. The plate can be cut to any size needed.

The steel plate should not be too thin or it will buckle over time. A good thickness is 6–8 mm. If the barbecue plate is larger than normal, increase the thickness or have steel rods welded onto the underside to prevent it bending or buckling.

PREPARATION AREA

Whether or not you incorporate preparation areas in the built unit, you will need to allow somewhere to place food and utensils during cooking. Most barbecue designs include a preparation area next to the hotplate on one or both sides. The size of this area can vary according to your needs and the space available. If the area is going to be used to store and prepare food before cooking as well as to serve guests, an area twice the size of the hotplate would be useful. If your barbecue setting includes a table where the cooked food, salads and utensils can be served, then a smaller preparation area would suffice.

When designing the preparation area, include an appropriate finish so that it will be easy to clean. Surfaces such as concrete and stone attract dirt and grease over time and would be better finished with wipe-clean surfaces such as ceramic tiles, sealed terracotta or slate.

WORKING HEIGHT

You should also consider the height of the preparation and cooking areas to avoid discomfort while cooking. An average height is between 850 and 950 mm, but if the main cook is particularly tall or short, you should adjust the height to suit. Eleven courses of brickwork will give a height of 825 mm while thirteen courses will give 975 mm.

STORAGE

Including preparation areas in your design often creates space for storage below. These storage areas can be left open to the weather or closed with doors. Shelves can be installed for utensils or equipment, or the space can be used to store wood or gas bottles. By providing covered storage for wood, you will ensure a dry supply of fuel in all weathers.

With gas-fired units, it is safer to store the gas bottle away from the burners and out of the weather. A small opening can be left in the brick jointing during construction so that

the gas line can be connected to the burners. Incorporate this into your planning and design stage or drill out a hole later. If doors are to be added to these areas, allow adequate ventilation in case of gas leakage. A gap at the top and bottom will allow air to circulate while protecting the area from the weather.

These areas are ideal for storing such things as the barbecue tools, perhaps hung on hooks on the backs of the doors, cleaning materials for the preparation areas, lava rocks or charcoal, smoking chips, dry matches, an ignition gun or even small garden tools and implements.

LOCATION

Deciding where to locate your barbecue can often be the most difficult part of building it. To get full use from your barbecue you need to locate it somewhere that is comfortable and convenient for cooking and entertaining.

Build the barbecue close to the house where you will have easy access to food, drinks and utensils. If you have an outdoor living area, perhaps with a pergola or patio, it will naturally form part of that. A barbecue placed apart from the living area isolates the cook from the guests and is less likely to be used. If you have to build the barbecue any distance from the house, plan paths or walkways to link them.

The choice of location will also be influenced by the prevailing weather conditions, as using the barbecue will be more comfortable if it is not exposed to strong winds, direct sunlight or excessive shade. You may also require some privacy from your neighbours. If you are planning a structure in the grounds of a listed building, check with your local council before beginning work.

You may find it helpful to sketch a plan of your house and backyard on paper (preferably to scale). On a separate piece of paper draw your proposed barbecue area to scale and cut it out. This cut-out can then be moved around the backyard plan until you find the best location.

SURROUNDING AREA

Any outdoor entertainment area, whether large or small, needs to be level, hard-wearing and without drainage problems. If you have a sloping site, consider terracing or constructing a deck.

The size of the overall barbecue area will be determined by the amount of space available, the number of people you want to accommodate and your budget, but you should always include enough room for the cook to work unhindered and for the guests to be served comfortably.

If you don't plan to have a barbecue very often and don't intend to have large parties, a small paved area or deck may be sufficient. On the other hand, if you plan to use the barbecue for large-scale entertaining, it may be worthwhile creating a more elaborate area with roofing, lighting, storage and preparation areas, seating and screening.

SURFACE MATERIAL

Select the surfacing material for the area carefully to provide an easy-care, comfortable and durable surround for the barbecue. Your choice will depend on the style of the house and landscaping, and your choice of material for the barbecue itself. For example, a barbecue constructed of sandstone blocks will often look best when it is surrounded by matching sandstone flagging.

Popular materials for surfacing the area around a barbecue include:
• brick pavers of clay or concrete
• house bricks
• concrete (either plain, stencilled or stamped)
• exposed aggregate
• slate
• tiles (terracotta or concrete)
• sandstone
• timber decking

If you use terracotta or slate, be aware that they provide a non-slip surface only if they are unsealed, but they are then likely to absorb grease from the barbecue.

Sandstone is porous and will show stains and discolour over time. It can be sealed, but you will need to check the manufacturer's instructions on a variety of sealants to select the best one for your paving.

Lawn is not a good choice for a barbecue surround as it tends to wear and remain wet underfoot. Loose materials such as gravel should also be avoided as they can be unstable. This is a decided disadvantage when you are carrying plates of food.

SHELTER

The barbecue area may need some protection from the weather, and the amount will depend on how exposed it is to wind and sun.

When looking at alternatives, consider the probable cost, ease of construction (and your level of skill) and how each will complement your existing house and garden landscape. The most important consideration is to create a functional, and yet comfortable, outdoor area.

Some possible structures are:
• roofing attached to the house;
• a separate cabana-type structure;
• a pergola or other open-timber framework which can be covered with light material such as lattice, canvas, overlapping fibreglass or metal sheeting;
• a trellis structure, perhaps used with a pergola to support climbing plants such as clematis;
• a screen or hedge of plants.

There are also less permanent means of shelter such as umbrellas. You may also be able to take advantage of existing shelter such as trees, parts of the building, fences or walls, thus reducing your costs.

LIGHTING

If you plan to use the barbecue area in the evenings you will need adequate lighting. Family and friends will want to see what they are eating,

and the cook will need to see what is being cooked. At the barbecue itself, a light directly overhead or directed onto the cooking area from the side is best. Fluorescent lighting casts fewer shadows, but an overhead spot onto the cooking and preparation surfaces will suffice.

Within the barbecue area, more subtle lighting can be used to create atmosphere and to highlight garden or landscaping features. Fixed permanent lighting must be installed by a qualified electrician or you may choose to use moveable garden lighting or portable floods, which can be run from a nearby power source.

Whatever you choose, it is important to decide about lighting during the planning stage so that electrical conduits can be run beneath any paving or concrete.

COSTS

The costs involved in the construction of a barbecue area depend on how elaborate it is. You will probably find that the cost of the barbecue itself will be minimal within the overall project budget.

Some of the features to include in your costing are:
• the barbecue itself
• retaining walls or screens
• paving or other surfacing
• any shade structure
• seating
• a lighting and power supply

Neat, accurate bricklaying is essential if you are to have a barbecue that looks attractive as well as adding to the amenities of your home.

Brickwork basics

Most built barbecues are constructed from bricks. Basic bricklaying is not difficult but it does require some practice to achieve a neat result.

SETTING OUT THE SLAB

1 Mark out the area for the concrete slab, ensuring the corners are at 90 degrees. Check them with a builders square or use the 3-4-5 method (see the box on page 16). When the area has been laid out, check the corners are at right angles by measuring the two diagonals: if they are the same length, then the area has been correctly laid out.

2 Excavate the area to a depth of 100 mm, removing grass and any other vegetation.

3 Form up the perimeter with timber formwork that will hold the concrete in position until it has hardened. For the formwork use long, straight pieces of timber held in place with a few pegs around the outside. Check the formwork is square and level before fixing it in position with nails and more pegs. Build in a slight crossfall to make it easier to hose down the slab once it is in use.

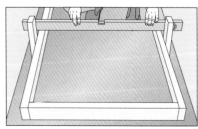

3 Form up the perimeter with timber formwork and check it for square and level before fixing it in position.

> ### TOOLS FOR BRICKLAYING
>
> - Measuring tape
> - String line
> - Spirit level
> - Builders square
> - Spade
> - Hammer
> - Steel mesh cutters or angle grinder
> - Shovel
> - Wheelbarrow
> - Wooden float
> - 75 mm edger
> - Coloured china pencil
> - Mortar board
> - Bricklaying trowel
> - Gauge rods (if needed)
> - Corner blocks
> - Club hammer and bolster
> - Scutch hammer
> - Jointing tool (optional)
> - Small brush
> - Sponge and bucket

THE 3-4-5 METHOD

From the corner point measure down one side 300 mm and down the other 400 mm (or you can use any multiples of these numbers, for example, 3 m and 4 m or 600 mm and 800 mm). The hypotenuse (or diagonal) should equal 500 mm (or the appropriate multiple) if you have made a right-angle triangle.

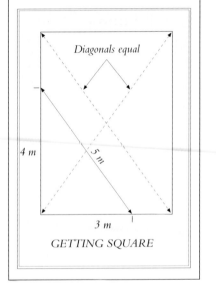

Diagonals equal

4 m

5 m

3 m

GETTING SQUARE

4 Lay a sheet of steel reinforcing mesh inside the formwork, making sure there is a 50 mm clearance around the edges. The mesh will increase the strength of the concrete and prevent it cracking at a later time. Support the mesh on mesh men to lift it to the centre of the slab.

THE CONCRETE
5 Prepare the concrete.
• If you are hand mixing the concrete, a mix of four parts coarse aggregate (gravel), two parts fine aggregate (sand) and one part cement (4:2:1) is sufficient. You will probably find 10 mm sized aggregate easiest to work. Mix these dry materials together with a shovel, form a well in the centre and then pour enough water into the well to achieve an even consistency.
• Ready-mixed concrete is delivered in quantities that increase by 0.2 m³. The required product standard is Gen 3 or ST4, each with a minimum amount of 20 kg cement per metre.

6 Pour the concrete into the formwork, using a spade or shovel to

4 Fit a sheet of steel reinforcing mesh inside the formwork, ensuring a 50 mm clearance around the edges.

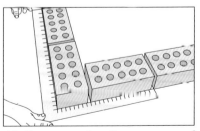

10 Lay out the first course of brickwork and use a builders square to check the corners are at 90 degrees.

spread it out. Keep the concrete level as you go and make sure that it is packed firmly under the steel reinforcing mesh.

7 Screed the concrete off by moving a piece of timber in a sawing motion across the top of the formwork. Use a hammer to tap along the side edge of the formwork to help settle the concrete edge and to prevent honeycombing (air pockets).

8 Use a wooden float to cream up the surface and pack the concrete at the edges hard. Then use an edger to roughly edge the slab and push the stones down.

9 Allow the concrete to dry to a point where only the surface is still workable. Refinish the surface and edge. Allow the concrete to cure, keeping it damp, for 2–3 days.

THE BRICKWORK

10 Using a straight edge as a guide, lay out the first course of brickwork. Allow for 10 mm joints between the bricks. Use a builders square to

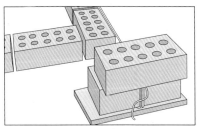

11 Set taut string lines along the bricks, allowing an extra 10 mm in height for the bed of mortar.

CONSTRUCTING A GAUGE ROD

Construct a gauge rod by placing a length of timber vertically against an existing 'quality' brick wall. Mark on the timber the location of the top of each brick course for the number of courses needed for your barbecue. Use a square to draw each mark around all sides of the gauge rod.

Alternatively, look at the height dimensions of brickwork provided on page 10 and transfer these onto the gauge rod.

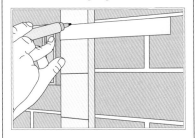

Mark on the timber the location of the top of each brick for the number of courses needed.

---

check the corners are at 90 degrees and measure the internal diagonal distance from corner to corner. The measurement should be the same both ways. Use a masonry pencil to mark the concrete along both sides of the brickwork, making guidelines to use later when laying the bricks.

11 Set taut string lines, allowing an extra 10 mm in height for the bed of mortar. Remove the bricks.

12 Unless you are an experienced bricklayer, construct gauge rods (see the box on page 17). Stand them vertically at each corner of the layout, fixing them in position with braces and pegs. Use a spirit level to make sure they are vertical both ways. As you work upwards, attach a string line for each course at the indicated mark.

13 Prepare a mortar mix. As bricks in a barbecue are affected by variations in temperature and should be able to expand and contract, use a mix ratio that is not too strong. Six parts sand, one part cement and one part lime (6:1:1) is ideal. You can also add a plasticizer to make the mix more workable. Mix the dry materials together thoroughly, perhaps in a wheelbarrow, and then add enough water to make a pliable mix with a consistency a bit like toothpaste. Mortar is useful for only about one and a half hours, so don't mix too much at once.

14 Transfer the mortar to a mortar board. To keep it soft and pliable you will have to continually work it backwards and forwards across the board with a trowel.

15 Spread the mix between the guidelines and lay the first course of bricks to the set string lines. On the trowel, pick up enough mortar to lay two bricks. Spread it on the slab (or existing brick course) at an even thickness of 15–20 mm. Pick up a brick, apply mortar to one end and position it on the bed of mortar, butting up to the last brick laid. Use the trowel to tap the brick into place so that the joints are a consistent thickness of 10 mm and then remove excess mortar. Check that the course is level with a spirit level and adjust by tamping if necessary.

16 Always lay the corners first and then fill in the wall between them. Lay the bricks so that the joints are staggered. To do this you will need to cut some bricks in half. Place a bolster at the appropriate place on the brick and hit it firmly with a club hammer. A scutch hammer can be used to chip off small pieces.

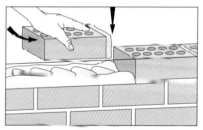

15 Pick up a brick, apply mortar to one end and place it on the bed of mortar, against the last brick laid.

17 As you build, use the spirit level to check that the walls are vertical and the courses are aligned.

MAKING A GOOD FIRE

If you are going to use solid fuel in your barbecue you need to plan the firebox carefully to ensure you have a fire that burns well.

Fire needs fuel and oxygen and the secret of a good fire is to get plenty of air to it. If the fuel is set on a grate, air can be drawn up from underneath and then into the flue and up the chimney. A chimney helps produce a good draught, which is why one is often incorporated into a barbecue.

The fire will stop burning when it runs out of fuel or when the air supply is cut off. Having some method of controlling the air supply, therefore, gives you greater control over the fire. In the Barbecue with two fires on page 32 dampers are set into the chimney to control the air flow, while the

Rustic-style barbecue on page 38 has a door across the firebox.

The opening to the flue should be two or three courses high, and the top should be level with the hotplate so that smoke is drawn up the chimney. If the opening is too small, smoke will build up and flow out of the front of the barbecue.

A metal damper is used to open and close off each half of the chimney in this barbecue (page 32).

17 As you build, use the spirit level to check that the walls are vertical and the steps are aligned.

18 To tie spur walls into the main wall, cut a notch halfway across and along the brick for the main wall and remove one-quarter of a brick for the spur wall. (Or use brick ties.)

19 Clean excess mortar off the bricks before it dries. Next day, wash the wall with water and a stiff brush. If necessary, wait several days and use a solution of 1 part hydrochloric acid

to 20 parts water to clean the brickwork. Always add the acid to the water (never water to acid), and wear protective goggles and gloves.

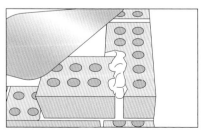

18 To join walls, cut a notch in the brick for one wall and remove one-quarter of a brick for the other wall.

The gas unit here is supported on the side slabs. You can ensure a neat fit by purchasing the unit and adjusting the layout before you begin to build.

Barbecue with storage

Basic bricklaying and carpentry skills are all that are required for this simple brick barbecue. The cooking area is flanked by terrazzo preparation areas and timber doors conceal the three storage areas below.

THE DESIGN

The basic structure consists of a wall with four projecting arms. In the centre bay a two-burner gas unit (divided into hotplate and grill and fuelled by bottled gas) is suspended between the side terrazzo slabs. A lava rock tray beneath the grill and

2 Following the bricklaying steps on pages 17–19 and the set-out diagram on page 23, construct the two end corners and two end arms to ten courses of brickwork. Use the spirit level to check for vertical and that the wall is flat.

3 Fix a string line in place between the corners, using two corner blocks. Also fix a string line across the front of the two end arms. These string lines can be moved upwards as each course of brickwork is completed. Complete the remainder of the back wall and the two centre arms to ten courses, building the centre arms at the same time as the back wall so that the relative heights can be checked as you work. Tie the centre arms into the back wall on the fourth and eighth courses (see step 18 on page 19). Allow the mortar to dry for 2–3 days before proceeding.

plate disperses the flame, providing an evenly heated cooking surface. A sand tray beneath the unit collects spills from the cooking surface.

On either side of the cooking area are terrazzo slab preparation areas. Timber doors close off the three storage areas below, which include space for the gas bottle in one side bay. An overhead light illuminates the cooking plate at night.

THE BRICKWORK
1 Set out and lay the 2500 x 800 mm concrete slab (see pages 15–17).

SIDE STORAGE AREAS
4 Cut the jambs and headers for the side bays, adjusting them to fit. Cut a 25 mm deep housing in each end of the headers. Rout a 15 x 15 mm

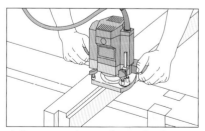

4 Rout a rebate along the bottom front edge of the header to prevent the door swinging inside.

21

MATERIALS★

- Concrete for slab: 0.25 m³ ready-mixed, *or* cement, sand and 10 mm aggregate
- 100 x 50 mm timber for formwork
- Timber pegs and nails
- A142M steel reinforcing mesh: 2300 x 800 mm
- Mesh men to support mesh
- 185 full bricks and 30 half bricks

- Cement, bricklayers sand, lime and plasticizer for mortar
- Two 860 x 740 mm terrazzo slabs and one 685 x 190 mm terrazzo slab (to fit behind gas unit)
- Two-burner gas barbecue unit with sand tray
- Lava rock tray and rocks
- Gas bottle, regulator and hoses

★ Finished size: 2240 x 665 mm and 790 mm high. Measurements are based on a brick size of 215 x 100 x 65 mm. Purchase the gas unit before starting to build and adjust the measurements to suit. Materials for doors are on page 24.

TOOLS

- Bricklaying tools (see page 15)
- Circular saw or tenon saw
- Pencil
- Hammer
- Drill with timber and masonry bits
- Screwdriver
- Cork sanding block
- Router (optional)
- Try square
- Rubber mallet

rebate along the bottom front edge of the headers for the top of the door to fit against. Glue and nail each header with 50 x 2.8 mm nails on top of the two jambs.

5 Place the frame in the opening, 50 mm in from the face of the brickwork. Using a pencil, mark two drill locations on each side, making sure the hole will be in the centre of

a brick. You do not want to drill into a joint. Drill the holes to accommodate 50 mm x 8 gauge countersunk screws. Place the frame in position, making sure it is vertical, and use a pencil to mark the position of the holes onto the brickwork. Remove the frame and use a masonry bit to drill 30 mm deep holes into the brickwork to accommodate plastic wall plugs. Tap the wall plugs into the brickwork before replacing the frame and fixing it in position using 50 mm screws.

6 Take two shelf supports. Place them against the side walls in one side bay, about 410 mm above the level of the concrete slab. Once again make sure that the drill location is in the centre of a brick. Drill the holes and fix the supports in the same way as the door jambs. Repeat with the other two shelf supports in the other side bay.

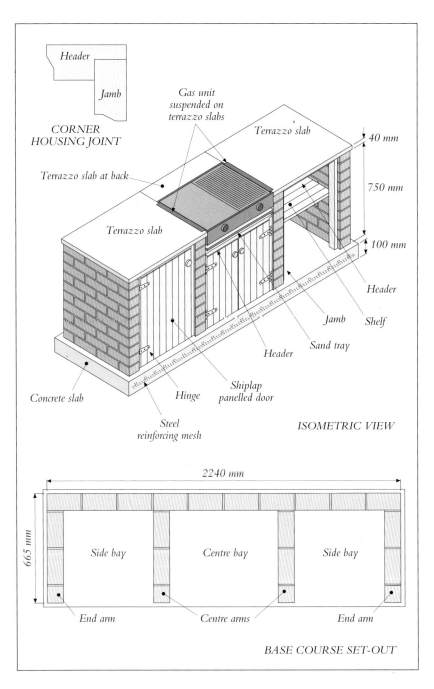

Header

Jamb

CORNER
HOUSING JOINT

Gas unit
suspended on
terrazzo slabs

Terrazzo slab

40 mm

750 mm

Terrazzo slab at back

100 mm

Terrazzo slab

Header

Jamb   Shelf

Sand tray

Header

Shiplap
panelled door

Concrete slab   Hinge

Steel
reinforcing mesh   ISOMETRIC VIEW

2240 mm

665 mm

Side bay   Centre bay   Side bay

End arm   Centre arms   End arm

BASE COURSE SET-OUT

23

MATERIALS FOR DOORS★

PART	MATERIAL	LENGTH	NO.
Header (side areas)	50 x 50 mm WRC	530 mm	2
Header (centre area)	50 x 50 mm WRC	640 mm	1
Jamb (side areas)	50 x 25 mm WRC	735 mm	4
Jamb (centre area)	50 x 25 mm WRC	585 mm	2
Tray support (back)	50 x 25 mm timber	640 mm	1
Shelf support	50 x 25 mm timber	450 mm	4
Ledger (side doors)	50 x 25 mm WRC	490 mm	4
Ledger (centre doors)	50 x 25 mm WRC	297 mm	4
Brace (side doors)	50 x 25 mm WRC	720 mm	2
Brace (centre doors)	50 x 25 mm WRC	540 mm	2
Tray rail	50 x 75 mm timber	450 mm	2
Cladding (side doors)	88 x 10 mm shiplap	710 mm	14
Cladding (centre doors)	88 x 10 mm shiplap	560 mm	10
Shelf	88 x 10 mm shiplap	530 mm	14

OTHER: Twenty plastic wall plugs for attaching timber frame to bricks; 50 x 2.8 mm galvanized round-head twist nails; 30 x 2 mm galvanized round-head twist nails; 50 mm x 8 gauge galvanized countersunk screws; eight hinges; four door knobs; four magnetic door latches; abrasive paper; finish of choice

★ Western red cedar (WRC) was used for all timberwork. The timber sizes given are nominal (see box on page 51). Adjust lengths to fit your structure.

CENTRE STORAGE AREA

7 Cut the pieces for the centre bay framework. The jambs reach to the top of the eighth course of bricks. Repeat the process in steps 4 and 5.

8 Cut the tray support piece to length. Drill holes and fix it on the back wall, 50 mm below the top of the header. Sit the tray rails on the support piece, butting them against the header. Nail them in place.

DOOR CONSTRUCTION

9 The doors are constructed to allow a 3 mm gap all round (the gap at the bottom provides air circulation for the storage areas within). The side doors on this unit are 710 x 490 mm while the centre doors are 560 x 297 mm, but adjust them to fit your unit. Cut shiplap panelling slightly longer than is required. For each door lay out the boards inside face up, butting them loosely together.

10 Cut the top and bottom ledgers to length. Square up the ends and fix them to the inside of the shiplap. Nail through the ledgers with 30 x 2 mm nails to fix each panel in place.

11 Place the diagonal brace in position: it should be angled from the bottom inside to the top outside and 40 mm in from each side. Mark the angles with a pencil and cut them. Fix the brace in place. Square up the top and bottom of the door and cut to the exact length required.

12 Lightly sand and paint or stain the doors. Fit a pair of hinges to each door centred 100 mm from top and bottom. This ensures that each hinge is fixed where the ledger is located. Fit door knobs at the height of the top ledger for strength. Fit magnetic door latches to complete the doors.

TO FINISH

13 Construct the shelves as for the doors, using shiplap and offcuts for ledgers (a diagonal brace is not needed). Place each shelf in position and fix it with 30 x 2 mm nails.

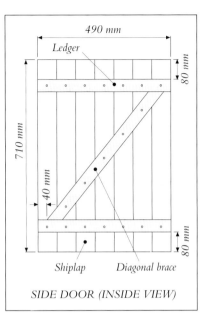

SIDE DOOR (INSIDE VIEW)

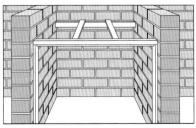

8 Fit the tray support piece to the back wall, sit the tray rails on it and fix them to the door header.

14 The large terrazzo slabs sit over the side bays while the small one fits behind the gas unit. To fit the slabs, spread mortar on top of the brickwork using a trowel. Ensure there is a good bed that will compress down to a thickness of about 10 mm. Lift each slab and place it carefully in position so that there is an even overlap all around (you will need a helper). Check that the distance between the slabs will accommodate the gas unit. Tamp the slabs into position with a rubber mallet and check for level in all directions. Allow to set and dry.

15 Drop the barbecue unit into position. Slide the sand tray beneath the unit on the timber rails. Connect the gas and light the barbecue.

Barbecue with rear screen

This gas-fired barbecue has a fake chimney, which forms part of an in-built screen that divides the barbecue from a covered eating area directly behind it and helps support a deck.

DESIGN

This barbecue unit of dry pressed brick with raked joints has a drop-in gas unit with grill and hotplate. The unit has five gas burners. On either side of the cooking area is a 525 x 920 mm preparation area covered with tiles, with storage areas for gas bottles and other equipment below.

The chimney is not functional as it does not open into the firebox, and it has been included for decorative

The back wall of this barbecue effectively divides open and covered entertaining areas but could also be used to screen off an unsightly view.

effect. It forms part of a rear screen with decorative metal grilles. In the photograph below the screen helps support a deck, which provides cover for a sunken eating area, but an extra two or three courses could be added to the top instead to make it suitable for any location.

BRICKLAYING

1 Set out and lay the 3000 x 700 mm area for the slab following the instructions on pages 15–17.

2 Following the bricklaying instructions on pages 17–19 and the

set-out diagram for this barbecue on page 28, build the end corners and end arms to a height of ten courses. Stretch a taut string line between the corners to use as a guide when laying the rest of the back wall. Keep an eye on the perpendicular joints, making sure that they stay straight. On the tenth course of the end arms lay only the outside row of bricks.

3 Complete the back wall, the two centre arms and the front wall up to the sixth course. Tie the fourth course of the centre arms into the back wall as shown on page 19.

4 Continue the brickwork, laying the back wall and the two centre arms to the ninth course, leaving the front wall open. Tie the arms to the back wall in the eighth course. Then lay the tenth course, but lay only the

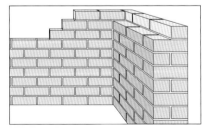

2 Build the end corners and end arms to ten courses, but on the tenth course of the arms lay only the outside row.

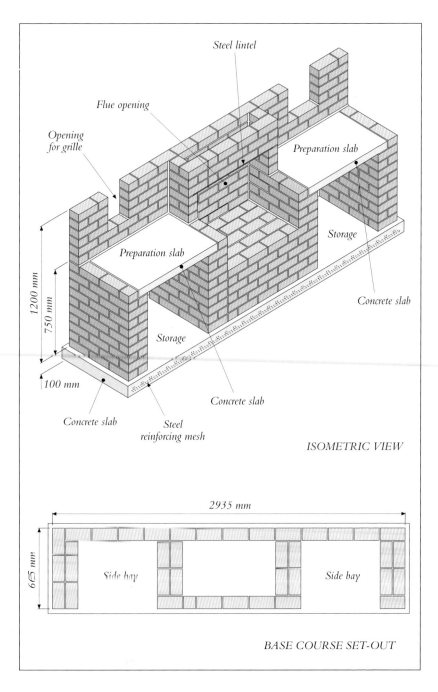

Steel lintel

Flue opening

Opening
for grille

Preparation slab

Preparation slab

Storage

Concrete slab

1200 mm

750 mm

100 mm

Storage

Concrete slab

Concrete slab

Steel
reinforcing mesh

ISOMETRIC VIEW

2935 mm

65 mm

Side bay

Side bay

BASE COURSE SET-OUT

MATERIALS★

- Concrete for ground slab: 0.25 m³ ready-mixed (extra 0.2 m³ if footing required for back wall), *or* cement, sand and 10 mm aggregate
- 100 x 50 mm timber for formwork
- Ten timber pegs
- A142M steel reinforcing mesh: 3200 x 700 mm and two 850 x 500 mm
- Cement, bricklayers sand, lime and plasticizer for mortar
- 427 full bricks and 32 half bricks (for sixteen courses)
- 90 x 8 mm steel lintel 960 mm long

- Two aluminium decorative grilles
- Tiles 1.6 m³
- 75 x 3.5 mm galvanized round-head nails
- Two 940 x 600 mm sheets fibre cement or marine plywood
- Concrete for preparation slabs: 0.12 m³
- Sand to fill firebox cavity
- Five-burner gas unit to fit
- Gas bottle with regulator and hose
- Timber 75 x 38 mm and 2935 mm long *or* two 90 x 8 mm lintels 400 mm long

★ Finished size: 2935 x 665 mm and 1200 mm high (based on a brick size of 215 x 100 x 65 mm).

inside row on the arms so as to make ledges. These ledges will support the concrete preparation slabs above the storage areas.

5 The chimney is built on the inside rows of the centre arms and its walls are only one brick thick. It projects in one brick length from the back wall. Lay the first two courses of the chimney sides as you build up the

back wall by another two courses to form the screen. Mark the positions of the grilles on the top of the bricks and leave space for them as you build higher (the grilles in this unit were one and a half bricks long and four bricks high).

6 Lay another course on the back wall and chimney sides and then place a 90 x 8 mm bar lintel in

4 On the tenth course lay only the inside row on the centre arms to make ledges for the concrete pads.

6 Place a lintel in position over the firebox and continue laying courses for the chimney and back wall.

Instead of a complete gas unit, this barbecue would work well with a hotplate and five-burner gas framework. Insert two 10 mm diameter rods across the firebox before laying the tenth course and rest a 12 mm thick hotplate on them. The gas burners are placed under the hotplate, supported on either side by concrete blocks or a couple of bricks.

position over the sides of the chimney to support the upper part of the chimney. Complete another three courses of brickwork (or more if you want the chimney and screen taller; if so, use 400 mm long lintels over the grille openings).

TO FINISH

7 Paint the grilles the desired colour. Each grille rests on two points which are recessed into the brickwork to hold the grilles in place. Drill two holes 10 mm deep into the bricks with a 10 mm masonry bit. Stand the grille in position. Fix a timber plate across the top of the back wall.

8 Fill the firebox cavity with sand, finishing 70 mm below the finished height to allow bricks to be placed on it. Tamp and lightly hose the sand to compact it. Screed the sand to provide a level surface. Lay the bricks over the area in a stretcher pattern and compact them with a piece of timber and a club hammer. Grout the joints with fine sand.

9 Form the concrete slabs for the preparation areas by placing a sheet of fibre cement or plywood on top of each side bay. Nail a 1 m length of 100 x 50 mm timber to the face of the board to contain the concrete and brace the centre of this cross-piece to support the weight of the concrete. Place an 850 x 500 mm sheet of steel mesh in the centre of the slab to prevent cracking. Mix and pour the concrete (see pages 16–17) and finish the slabs with the wooden float. Allow to cure for 2–3 days.

10 Fix tiles to the concrete surface to make an easy-to-clean surface (see the box opposite).

11 The gas bottle is safest stored in one of the side storage areas away from the flames. If necessary, drill a 12 mm diameter hole through the brickwork for the gas line.

12 Position the gas unit, connect the gas and light the barbecue.

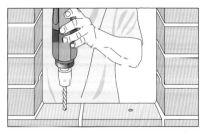

7 For the grilles drill two holes 10 mm deep into the brickwork with a 10 mm masonry bit.

LAYING CERAMIC TILES

1 Tiles are normally sold by the square metre, so calculate the amount you will need, including about 10 per cent extra to allow for breakage. The concrete base should be four weeks old before you start.

2 Ensure the surface to be tiled is completely clean. An ideal solution for cleaning concrete is one part hydrochloric acid to six parts water. Always add acid to water and wear goggles and gloves.

3 Lay out the tiles on the area to be covered. Adjust them to minimize the number of tiles that will have to be cut and so that the cut tiles are at the back or side edges of the area. Use a pencil to mark the cut on the back of the tile, allowing for joints, score along the line, place a nail under the line and snap down to break the tile.

4 Use a spatula to place the mortar or adhesive on the surface. A sand and cement mortar is fine, although prepared tiling adhesives are easier to use. With a notched trowel, spread mortar over 1 m^2 at a time. The trowel makes ridges that improve the grip on the tile.

5 Place the tiles in the mortar and settle them with a twist of the hand to remove air bubbles. Use nylon spacing crosses to achieve constant joint widths.

6 Gently clean off excess mortar before it dries, using a damp sponge and rinsing it frequently.

7 Leave the tiles for at least 24 hours and then apply grout with a rubber squeegee, working the grout well into the joints. Use a sponge to wipe off excess grout before it sets.

8 Wait 24 hours and then polish the surface of the tiles with a soft, dry cloth or crumpled newspaper.

8 Fill the firebox cavity with sand, add a layer of bricks and compact them. Fill the joints with fine sand.

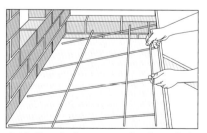

9 Nail a timber across the face of the preparation area to retain the concrete, and place steel mesh in the centre.

The chimney on this barbecue can draw smoke from one or both fires at the same time and has a directional cap to direct smoke away from the cooking area. A custom-made hinged stainless steel cover fits over the hotplate.

Barbecue with two fires

This barbecue is fuelled by two wood fires located at either end, so that the cook does not have to stand in front of the fire while cooking and can instead work at the large tiled area between the hotplate and chargrill plate. The unusual design does mean a little more work in construction.

- Bricklaying tools (see page 15)
- Angle grinder with masonry blade for cutting tiles

The chimney can draw smoke from either fire or from both at the same time. It is divided down the centre and has metal dampers that open and close the flues as required. A stainless steel cap sits on top of the chimney to direct smoke away from the cooking area.

A custom-made hinged stainless steel cover fits over the hotplate. This protects the plate when it is not in use, but can also be used when smoking or baking foods.

BRICKLAYING

1 Mark out the 2650 x 1250 mm area for the concrete slab and lay the concrete following the instructions on pages 15–17.

2 Follow the bricklaying instructions on pages 17–19 and the set-out diagram on page 35 to construct both ends of the front and back walls to a height of five courses.

3 Fill in the double brick walls to a height of five courses, at the same time building the dividing wall in the chimney and the two cross-walls. Make sure they are laid square to the front and back walls and that the chimney dividing wall is exactly in the centre of the chimney. Tie them in at least every fourth course by

DESIGN
This large unit is constructed of dry-pressed brick with flush jointing. It is fuelled by wood fires located at either end of the structure. One fire heats a large hotplate and the other a chargrill plate, allowing a choice of cooking styles, or two cooks can work at the one time to cater for a large group. The tiled preparation area is located between the hotplate and grill.

MATERIALS*

- Concrete for ground slab: 0.34 m^3 ready-mixed, *or* cement, sand and 10 mm aggregate
- 100 x 50 mm timber for formwork
- Timber pegs and nails
- A142M steel reinforcing mesh: 2600 x 1200 mm, 500 x 585 mm and two 790 x 585 mm
- Tie wire and mesh men
- Cement, bricklayers sand, lime and plasticizer for mortar
- 630 bricks
- Two steel lintels 655 x 90 x 8 mm
- Four steel lintels 300 x 90 x 8 mm
- Steel lintel 1130 x 90 x 8 mm

- Steel lintel 435 x 90 x 8 mm
- 5 mm thick fibre cement sheeting: 525 x 665 mm and two pieces 890 x 665 mm
- Concrete for preparation and two firebox slabs: 0.18 m^3
- Hotplate 865 x 525 x 12 mm
- Grill plate 420 x 525 mm
- Stainless steel hotplate cover
- Two steel flue dampers 345 x 115 x 5 mm with handles
- Stainless steel chimney cap
- 2.3 m^2 tiles
- Tile fixative
- Grout for tiles

* Finished size: 2475 x 890 mm; height of cooking surface 810 mm, total height including chimney 1620 mm (based on brick dimensions of 215 x 100 x 65 mm).

notching out and overlapping the brickwork as shown in step 18 on page 19. When the mortar has set, position a 655 x 90 x 8 mm steel lintel on the fifth course at either end of the barbecue unit so that it sits across the opening.

4 Lay the sixth course right around the structure but at the ends where the firebox slabs will go use only a single skin of brickwork.

5 Once the brickwork has set, place a base of fibre cement sheeting over

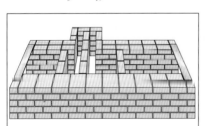

3 Fill in the double brick walls to five courses and position a steel lintel across the opening at each end.

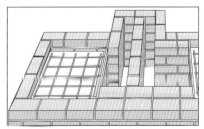

5 Set in place a base of fibre cement sheet and steel mesh ready to pour the concrete for the firebox slabs.

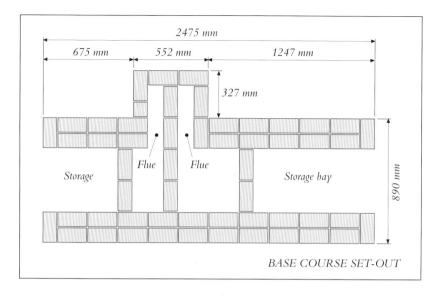

2475 mm

675 mm   552 mm   1247 mm

327 mm

Storage

Flue   Flue

Storage bay

890 mm

BASE COURSE SET-OUT

the storage bays, with timber supports below. Add steel mesh. Mix concrete for the two firebox slabs as described on pages 16–17, finishing at the height of the sixth course. Leave the slabs to set.

6 Lay the 1130 x 90 x 8 mm lintel between the slabs and immediately behind the front double brick wall. This will support a third row of bricks under the central preparation

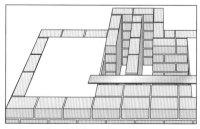

6 Lay the 1130 x 90 x 8 mm lintel between the slabs and immediately behind the front double brick wall.

area so as to narrow the flue and help to move smoke from the fires towards the chimney.

7 Lay the ends of the front and rear walls to nine courses, at the same time laying bricks for the seventh course across the ends over the lintels but leaving the eighth and ninth courses open for the firebox openings (see diagram on page 37). Set string lines off the ends and fill in the middle of the walls, including the chimney and chimney dividing wall.

8 Place two 300 x 90 x 8 mm lintels side by side over the firebox opening at each end. Place a 435 x 90 x 8 mm lintel across the two flue openings so the tenth course of the rear wall can continue straight across. Lay the tenth course around the outside in single brick only, as this

will contain the concrete slab. Allow the brickwork to set.

9 Place a 890 x 665 mm piece of fibre cement sheeting on top of the ninth course of brickwork where the central slab will go. Using 100 x 50 mm timber, form up the two sides to contain the concrete at the edge of the hotplate and grill areas. Place a piece of steel mesh inside the formwork. Cover this area with concrete to the height of the tenth course. Allow it to set before removing the formwork.

10 Continue the chimney to the height of twenty courses, using gauge rods as in step 12 on page 18. Construct the rib in the centre using bricks laid on edge so that each half of the chimney is exactly 135 mm wide. Tie the rib to the outer chimney walls every third course by notching bricks or using metal brick ties. On the front face omit the mortar between courses 17 and 18 to exactly the width of the inside openings. This is to allow the metal dampers to slide in and out, opening

and closing each flue as required and controlling the burn rate of each fire.

TO FINISH
11 The width available for the hotplate and grill is 665 mm. If your hotplate and grill are narrower, you can make the opening narrower by cutting bricks and mortaring them inside the edge bricks of the hotplate and grill areas. The width of the top surface around the hotplate and grill can also be varied to suit the tiles you are using.

12 Tile the surface of the brickwork and concrete preparation slab (see the box on page 31).

13 Place the hotplate and chargrill on the supporting brickwork. The optional stainless steel chimney cap and hotplate cover can be made at most metal fabrication or engineering shops. Fix the cap with four screws into plastic plugs.

14 Before using the barbecue, fire up both ends, open the flues and check the chimney works correctly.

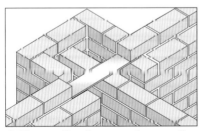

8 Place a lintel across the two flue openings so the tenth course of the rear wall can continue straight across.

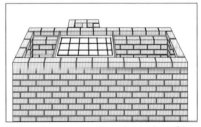

9 For the preparation slab, place fibre cement on top of the ninth course, form up the two sides and add mesh.

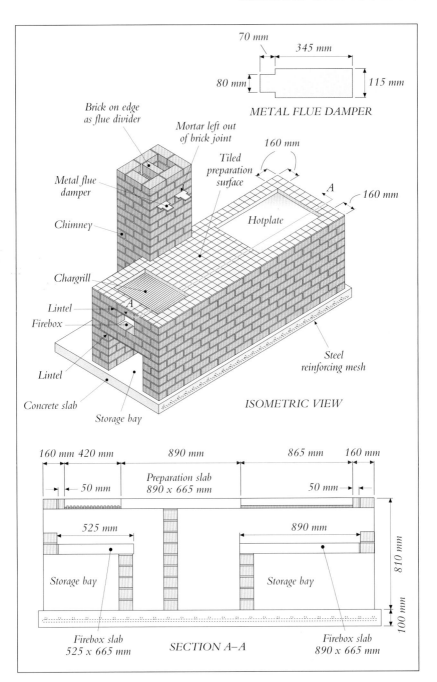

70 mm
345 mm
80 mm
115 mm
METAL FLUE DAMPER

Brick on edge
as flue divider

Mortar left out
of brick joint

Tiled
preparation
surface

160 mm

Metal flue
damper

A

160 mm

Chimney

Hotplate

Chargrill

Lintel

A

Firebox

Lintel

Steel
reinforcing mesh

Concrete slab

Storage bay

ISOMETRIC VIEW

160 mm 420 mm   890 mm   865 mm   160 mm

50 mm   Preparation slab
               890 x 665 mm   50 mm

525 mm   890 mm

810 mm

Storage bay   Storage bay

100 mm

Firebox slab
525 x 665 mm   SECTION A–A   Firebox slab
                                       890 x 665 mm

Built from dry-pressed bricks laid in a rustic style, this unusual barbecue includes an area for chargrilling, a removable hotplate and a rotisserie unit, as well as a sink with running water and ample storage space.

Rustic-style barbecue

This barbecue doesn't have a chimney, but the firebox has a door to control airflow and burn rate. The structure is full of unusual features and will challenge more adventurous do-it-yourselfers.

DESIGN

This barbecue is fired with wood, giving a smoked taste to the food as there is no chimney. The firebox does, however, have an adjustable door to control the airflow and burn rate of the fire. Beneath the firebox and tiled preparation areas are storage

grass and other vegetation from the area. Position a 50 mm PVC pipe to carry waste from the sink. It should project at least 200 mm above the slab level for ease of connection later. Lay the concrete slab (see pages 16–17).

2 Following the bricklaying instructions on pages 17–19 and the set-out diagram on page 42, set out and lay the base course.

THE BRICKWORK

3 Construct the two end arms and corners to eight courses.

4 Set string lines back and front and use them as guidelines to lay the rear wall and centre arms. When course 4 is completed erect braces (300 mm high) against the inside faces of the inner arms to carry the overhang of brickwork in course 5. To do this, position bricks on edge one above the other against each end of the arm and lay a timber on top. Lay course 5 so that the inner row (except the front brick) overlaps the timber support by 50 mm. Fill the gap

areas. The left-hand preparation area contains a sink with tap.

The cooking area has a grill for chargrilling, and aluminium strips can be placed over the bars to control the flames or a removable hotplate can be placed on it. The two centre arms are built higher to support a rotisserie which has two height settings and is driven by an electric motor.

LAYING OUT

1 Mark out the 4000 x 1000 mm area for the concrete slab. Excavate to a depth of 100 mm, removing

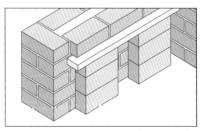

4 Lay course 5 to overlap on the inside faces of the inner arms and fill the gap with mortar.

MATERIALS★

- Concrete for base slab: 0.4 m³ ready-mixed, or cement, sand and 10 mm aggregate
- 100 x 50 mm timber for formwork
- Timber pegs and nails
- A142M reinforcing mesh: 3650 x 810 mm, 810 x 690 mm, 810 x 600 mm and pieces for around sink
- Mesh men
- Cement, bricklayers sand, lime and plasticizer for mortar
- 660 bricks
- Concrete for firebox and preparation slabs: 0.26 m³
- 5 mm thick fibre cement sheeting: 890 x 790 mm and two 890 x 685 mm
- Capping pavers for central arms
- 1.8 m² tiles and grout
- Six steel lintels 960 x 90 x 8 mm
- Sink 415 x 330 mm

- Water tap plus 12 mm copper pipe and fittings
- 2000 x 50 mm PVC drainage pipe and fittings
- Rotisserie unit including motor, skewer and 300 mm of notched angle iron
- Two 230 mm lengths of 12 mm galvanized water pipe
- Twelve grill bars 150 x 600 mm to cover a 810 x 532 mm area in two metal frames
- Hotplate with handles 600 x 450 x 8 mm
- Aluminium drop-down draft door 150 x 825 mm
- 3 mm aluminium strip 825 x 60 mm
- Two hinges and sixteen pop rivets for firebox door flap
- 20 x 20 mm angle iron for fire grate and hotplate
- Silicone for waterproofing sink

★ Finished size: 3590 x 890 mm; height at centre arms 1200 mm (based on brick dimensions of 215 x 100 x 65 mm). For materials for doors see page 44.

between the rows with mortar. The subsequent courses are set back but will hold the overhang in place. The bracing can be removed when the brickwork is dry. This overhang will be used to support the firebox slab. Complete the brickwork to course 8.

5 Construct timber formwork to contain the firebox slab. Cut a piece of fibre cement sheeting to fit exactly into the base of the opening. Brace it in position to prevent it flexing under the weight of the concrete.

Fix a 100 x 50 mm timber across the front. Add steel mesh and concrete.

6 Position timber braces 600 mm high, as in step 4, on either side of the side bays (that is, the inner faces of the end arms and the outer faces of the inner arms). These will carry overhangs of brickwork in course 9 to support the preparation slabs. Position the six steel lintels across the front openings with two in each section, one behind the other. These will carry two rows of brickwork two courses high.

7 Lay course 9, overlapping the bricks on each side of the side bays as in step 4 and laying a double row of brickwork across the lintels.

8 Lay course 10 on the end arms, but lay only the outside row so as to accommodate the slab. In the cooking bay set timber braces in position at the sides and back to support brick overhangs in course 10. This three-sided overhang of 50 mm will support the grill frame. Cut three bricks lengthwise to 40 mm to fit in the back wall where the course 10 bricks will be indented.

9 Complete course 10, but with the front wall in the side bays only a single brick thick to allow for the slabs.

10 Construct the timber formwork to contain the concrete preparation slabs. Cut pieces of fibre cement sheeting to fit exactly into the base of the two openings and brace them. In the left-hand bay form up a 415 x 330 mm 'island' where the sink will go (adjust the size to fit your sink). Mark and then cut out the opening

TOOLS

- Bricklaying tools (see page 15)
- Angle grinder with masonry blade for cutting tiles
- Circular saw or tenon saw
- Jigsaw
- Drill with timber and masonry bits
- Screwdriver
- Cork sanding block
- Router (optional)
- Welding equipment

with a jigsaw. Form up the four sides of the opening with 100 x 50 mm timber and nail into position.

11 Drill a 15 mm hole in the rear wall of the brickwork for a 12 mm copper water pipe to pass through. Position the copper pipe through the wall and the proposed slab.

12 Place steel reinforcing mesh in each formed-up area. Mix and pour the concrete. Finish the slabs with a wooden float to produce a rough textured surface that will provide better adhesion for the tiles. Allow to

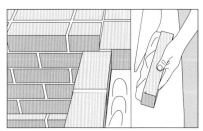

8 Lay course 10, including the cut bricks in the rear wall where the bricks were indented.

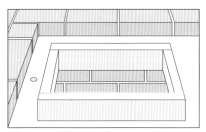

10 In the left-hand preparation area form up a 415 x 330 mm 'island' where the sink will be placed.

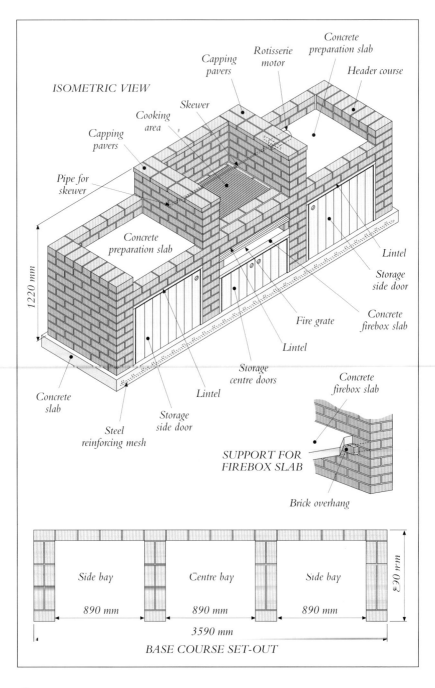

ISOMETRIC VIEW

Concrete preparation slab

Rotisserie motor

Concrete preparation slab

Header course

Capping pavers

Skewer

Cooking area

Capping pavers

Pipe for skewer

Concrete preparation slab

1220 mm

Lintel

Storage side door

Concrete firebox slab

Fire grate

Lintel

Storage centre doors

Concrete slab

Lintel

Storage side door

Steel reinforcing mesh

Concrete firebox slab

SUPPORT FOR FIREBOX SLAB

Brick overhang

BASE COURSE SET-OUT

Side bay

Centre bay

Side bay

890 mm

890 mm

890 mm

3590 mm

590 mm

cure for 2–3 days before stripping off the formwork.

13 Complete the two end arms and back wall, laying the final course 12 header style. Complete the two centre arms and centre back wall to a height of fifteen courses, halfway back in each arm inserting a 230 mm length of water pipe in the joint above course 13 for the rotisserie. Add a capping of pavers to the centre arms and back.

FINISHING THE UNIT

14 Tile the surface of the two preparation areas and the front of the cooking area to make them easy to clean (see the box on page 31).

15 Have a plumber install the sink and tap. When seating the sink on the tiles, run a bead of silicone around the edge for waterproofing.

16 Using 20 x 20 mm angle iron construct a framework 810 mm long x 532 mm wide for the fire grate. Prepare mitred corners and weld them together. Place 6 x 150 mm grates across the framework and cover them with chicken-wire mesh to form a grate. Place bricks on edge at either side of the firebox slab and rest the grate on them.

17 To construct a drop-down door for the firebox, take a 825 x 60 mm strip of aluminium and pop rivet two hinges to it 20 mm from each end. Then rivet a 825 x 150 mm piece of aluminium to the hinges to create the 'flap' or door.

18 On the 60 mm wide strip, mark and drill two 5 mm holes in the centre and 300 mm from each end. Position the strip in front of the firebox slab. Mark the position of the holes with a pencil. Remove the strip and drill two holes into the face of the slab with a masonry bit. Plug them with plastic lugs. Screw the aluminium strip, with the 'flap' attached, to the front of the slab. Fix a latch with notches on one side of the flap to allow it to be adjusted.

19 Using 20 x 20 mm angle iron construct a second framework 810 mm long x 532 mm wide for the cooking plate, again with welded mitred corners. Sit the framework on the brick ledges in the cooking area and insert 6 x 150 mm grates across the frame to form a grill. Sit the hotplate on top of these 'grill bars'.

20 Mark the position for the bracket that will hold the rotisserie motor. This is on the outside of the right-hand centre arm, with the centre of the drive shaft exactly over the hole formed by the galvanized pipe so that the removable skewer will pass through the hole and slot exactly into the drive mechanism. Drill holes and fix the bracket into position with expansion bolts. Use these bolts to fix the notched support angle to the brickwork on the inside of the arm so it provides support for the skewer.

MATERIALS FOR DOORS★

Part	Material	Length	No.
Outer jamb (side area)	75 x 38 mm WRC	570 mm	4
Outer header (side area)	75 x 38 mm WRC	855 mm	2
Inner jamb (side area)	75 x 38 mm WRC	557 mm	4
Inner header (side area)	75 x 38 mm WRC	800 mm	2
Outer jamb (centre area)	75 x 38 mm WRC	350 mm	2
Outer header (centre area)	75 x 38 mm WRC	855 mm	1
Inner jamb (centre area)	75 x 38 mm WRC	337 mm	2
Inner header (centre area)	75 x 38 mm WRC	800 mm	1
Catch plate (side area)	50 x 16 mm WRC	567 mm	2
Side rail (side door)	75 x 50 mm WRC	553 mm	4
Top/bottom rail (side door)	75 x 50 mm WRC	623 mm	4
Side rail (centre door)	75 x 50 mm WRC	327 mm	4
Top/bottom rail (centre door)	75 x 50 mm WRC	250 mm	4
Panelling (side door)	110 x 10 mm shiplap	538 mm	16
Panelling (centre door)	110 x 10 mm shiplap	320 mm	8

OTHER: 30 x 20 mm galvanized round-head nails; 50 mm x 8 gauge screws; twelve timber fixing plugs; twelve 90 x 10 mm screws; eight door hinges; four bolts or latches; four handles; abrasive paper; wood filler; finish of choice

★ Western red cedar (WRC) is used for all frame components. Timber sizes given are nominal (see page 51). Adjust the lengths to fit your structure.

ADDING THE DOORS

21 Cut the outer jambs and header for the side storage areas, adjusting the lengths to fit your barbecue. Butt the header on top of the two jambs and nail them together. Position the frame in the opening.

22 Cut the inner jambs and header. Cut a 15 mm deep corner housing in each end of the header. Glue and nail the jambs to the header. Position the second frame 15 mm inside the first to create a rebate for the door. Glue and nail the two frames together.

23 Recess the jambs 10 mm from the front of the brickwork. Drill two 8 mm holes through each double jamb and mark the points on the brickwork. Remove the framework and drill into the brickwork with a

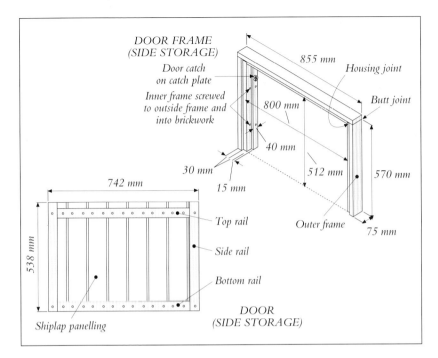

**DOOR FRAME
(SIDE STORAGE)**

Door catch
on catch plate

Inner frame screwed
to outside frame and
into brickwork

855 mm

Housing joint

Butt joint

800 mm

40 mm

30 mm

742 mm

15 mm

512 mm

570 mm

538 mm

Top rail

Side rail

Bottom rail

Outer frame

75 mm

Shiplap panelling

**DOOR
(SIDE STORAGE)**

masonry bit. Plug the holes with timber or plastic plugs and fix the frame in place with 50 mm x 8 gauge screws. Nail a catch plate to the inner edge of the frame on the side where the door catch will be fixed.

24 Fit a framework to the centre storage area in the same way but omit the catch plate. In the barbecue shown on page 38, the jambs were inset further and made thicker to accommodate the unusual hinges.

25 The side doors are 538 mm high by 742 mm long and the centre doors each 327 mm high by 370 mm long. Measure the openings in your barbecue, allow for a 3 mm gap all

round and adjust the door sizes as necessary. Cut the shiplap panelling slightly longer than will be required. Then cut the top, bottom and side rails to length.

26 Butt-joint the rails together with the bottom rail flush with the bottom of the side rails and the top rail 50 mm down from the top. Glue and nail them together. Using 30 x 2 mm round-head nails, fix the panelling to the framework. Punch in the nails and fill the holes with wood filler. Square up the ends of the panelling and trim it to the correct length.

27 Fix the hinges, latches and handles to the doors.

On either side of this barbecue a brick wall with two arms supports a slatted seat that can double as a preparation area. The surrounding area is surfaced with clay pavers laid in a herringbone pattern.

Barbecue with decorative chimney

This neat gas-fired barbecue incorporates a non-functional chimney but requires only basic bricklaying skills. The storage area is topped with slate and closed with timber doors.

MATERIALS*

- Concrete for slab: 0.2 m³ ready-mixed, *or* cement, sand and 10 mm aggregate
- 100 x 50 mm timber for formwork
- Timber pegs and nails
- A142M steel reinforcing mesh: 1500 x 700 mm
- Tie wire
- Cement, bricklayers sand, lime and plasticizer for mortar
- 400 bricks (extruded bricks were used for the barbecue shown opposite)

- 25 paving bricks
- Flat steel lintel 1100 x 90 x 8 mm
- Flat steel lintel 445 x 90 x 8 mm
- Five pieces of slate 217 x 100 mm
- Stainless steel cover lid
- Five-burner gas unit
- Natural gas fuel line, stopcock and pressure regulator
- Two 420 mm lengths of steel angle to support gas unit
- Four 50 mm expansion bolts

---

* Finished size: 1462 x 665 mm without chimney; height of arms 1050 mm; chimney 552 x 327 mm and 2100 mm high (based on brick measurements of 215 x 100 x 65 mm). For door materials see page 50.

THE DESIGN

This barbecue is built with extruded bricks and ironed joints to accommodate gas burners that are fuelled by natural gas. There is a non-functional chimney, included for decorative effect, and a storage space below the cooking area is closed with double timber doors. The firebox is paved with slate. A custom-made stainless steel cover is placed over the gas burners when they are not in use.

TOOLS

- Bricklaying tools (see page 15)
- Circular saw
- Drill and drill bits
- Screwdriver
- Cork sanding block
- Router (optional)
- Chisels
- Tenon saw
- Sash cramps

BRICKLAYING

1 Mark out and prepare the 1560 x 750 mm area for the concrete slab and the 575 x 375 mm slab area for the chimney (see pages 15–17).

2 Following the bricklaying instructions on pages 17–19 and the set-out diagram opposite, lay three courses, which includes the front, sides, back and chimney, tying in the chimney at the third course (and every third course hereafter).

3 Lay the next six courses for the sides, back and chimney, but not the front as you need to create the opening for the storage area. At the end of the ninth course, place the 1100 mm lintel across the opening at the front to create a header above the doorway. Lay course number ten, including across the front.

4 Lay the next three courses, but again leave the front open to create the firebox.

5 Construct the remaining fifteen courses of the chimney. To create a flue opening, leave out courses 14 and 15 at the front of the chimney and place the 445 mm lintel across the opening. You will find it easier to lay the upper courses of the chimney if you brace two gauge rods in place and follow them rather than string lines. Constantly check with a spirit level as you work to make sure that the chimney is vertical.

6 To cap the holes in the top of the extruded bricks, use brick pavers as the final course on the unit. Alternatively, you can fill the holes with mortar or cover them with tiles or slate.

7 Using expansion bolts, fix a 420 mm length of steel angle to each side of the firebox to support the gas unit. The precise positioning of the angle will depend on the size of your gas unit. In this barbecue the angle was positioned 230 mm below the bottom of the flue opening and waterproof adhesive was used to glue paving bricks onto each piece of steel angle, to provide extra support for the gas unit.

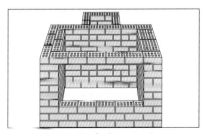

3 At the end of the ninth course, place a lintel across the opening and lay course number ten.

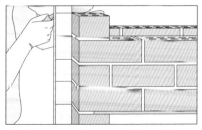

5 Construct the remaining fifteen courses of the chimney using two gauge rods as a guide.

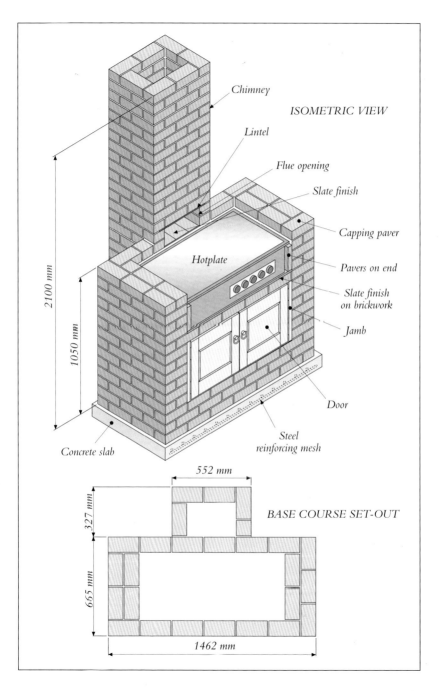

Chimney

ISOMETRIC VIEW

Lintel

Flue opening

Slate finish

Capping paver

Hotplate

Pavers on end

Slate finish
on brickwork

Jamb

2100 mm

1050 mm

Door

Steel
reinforcing mesh

Concrete slab

552 mm

327 mm

BASE COURSE SET-OUT

665 mm

1462 mm

MATERIALS FOR DOORS*

Part	Material	Length	Width	No.
Jamb	100 x 38 mm WRC	450 mm		2
Door stile	100 x 38 mm WRC	464 mm		4
Door rail	150 x 38 mm WRC	468 mm		4
Door panel	6 mm waterproof plywood	223 mm	305 mm	2

OTHER: Epoxy adhesive; abrasive paper; 3 m of beading; four plastic wall plugs; 25 x 1 mm panel pins; 50 mm x 8 gauge screws; four hinges and screws; two latches and screws; two handles; finish of choice

* Western red cedar (WRC) is used for all timber components. Timber sizes given are nominal (see box opposite). Adjust the lengths to suit your structure.

8 To cap the holes in the extruded bricks above the storage area and at the base of the flue, mortar pieces of slate in place.

ADDING THE DOORS

9 Cut the jambs to length and fix them to each side of the opening by drilling holes in the brickwork. Plug the holes with plastic wall plugs before fixing the jambs with screws.

10 Measure the width of the opening inside the frame and subtract 10 mm to allow a 3 mm gap between the doors and the jambs. Measure the height of the opening, subtract 6 mm to allow a 3 mm gap top and bottom. Divide the width by 2 to find the size of each door.

11 Cut four stiles 20 mm longer than the height. Cut two top and two bottom rails 20 mm longer than the width. Mark the overall height on the stiles.

12 Prepare mortise and tenon joints with tenons on the ends of the rails and mortises through the stiles inside the height marks. Cut them with a tenon saw and chisel. Glue the joints together with epoxy adhesive and hold them tight with sash cramps. Check them for square and adjust as required. Leave them to dry. Saw off the protruding tenon.

13 Sand the frame. Cut a 10 mm wide and 12 mm deep rebate around the inside face with a router, and square the corners with a chisel.

14 Cut and fit the door panels into the rebates. Cover the join on the outside face with beading. Nail it in position with 25 x 1 mm panel pins. Cut the stiles flush with the rails and plane the doors to fit (allowing a 3 mm clearance all round).

15 Fit hinges to each door. Fit handles and latches; attach the doors.

TO FINISH

16 Install the gas burner unit into the firebox area by sitting it on the paving bricks or directly onto the steel angle. Connect the gas and light the barbecue.

17 Make a protective stainless steel lid to cover the gas burners as well as the firebox area, or have one made to your specifications at an engineering, sheet metal or air-conditioning workshop. The cover should have a reasonable pitch so that water will run off it.

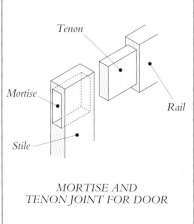

MORTISE AND TENON JOINT FOR DOOR

TIMBER

TIMBER FOR OUTDOOR USE

Timber used outdoors must be able to withstand the elements. Among possible choices are treated pine, Western red cedar and hardwood. All will require some type of protective finish, usually paint for treated pine, but natural oil finish will enhance the appearance of more attractive timbers.

TIMBER CONDITIONS

Timber is sold in three conditions:
- sawn or rough sawn
- planed, either planed all round (PAR), planed on two sides (P2S) or double planed
- moulded (planed to a specific profile for decorative purposes)

Most planed timbers are sold using the same nominal dimensions as sawn timber, for example 100 x 50 mm, although the surfaces have been machined down to a flat, even width and thickness so that the piece will actually measure 91 x 41 mm. Similarly, a planed 75 x 38 mm timber would actually measure 66 x 30 mm.

TIMBER LENGTHS

Prepared timber is sold in stock lengths, beginning at 0.9 m and increasing by 300 mm to 1.2 m, 1.9 m and so on. Short lengths and offcuts are also usually available.

TREATED TIMBER

Treated timber is sold in its finished size. Some of the available sizes are:

70 x 35 mm	70 x 45 mm
90 x 45 mm	90 x 90 mm
120 x 45 mm	

Pit barbecue

This is a version of the traditional campfire. The fire is contained within a brick pit set in a mosaic-paved square. Food is cooked on a campfire unit that fits into a pipe in the base of the pit.

DESIGN

The fire is contained within a pit that is constructed from bricks laid in a circle to create a 'well', which is capped with pool coping to form a neat edge. The pit is set within a square of pavers with mosaic infill.

The food is cooked on a steel plate that is supported on a steel pole. This also holds a separate grill and a hook for a billycan. All can be rotated around the pole and over the fire as required. Once the cooking is completed, the pole can be lifted out, the fire stoked and the guests can enjoy a contained open fire.

Before beginning this project, do check with your local council to see if you live in a smoke-free zone.

CREATING THE PIT

1 Decide how to drain the pit so it doesn't fill with water. If the base is above other points in the yard, run a pipe from the base to a low spot. If you have sandy soil, make holes in the slab for water to soak through, or you can make a lid for the pit.

MATERIALS*

- Concrete for base slab: 0.16 m³ ready-mixed, *or* cement, sand and 10 mm aggregate
- Concrete for top collar 0.2 m³
- A142M steel reinforcing mesh: 600 x 600 mm and four pieces 1450 x 200 mm
- Mesh men
- Cement, bricklayers sand, lime and plasticizer for mortar
- 66 bricks
- 25 clay pool coping stones
- 50 paving bricks

- Packing sand for backfilling the wall and beneath the paving
- Aggregate for drainage
- Permanent marking pen and coloured chinagraph pencil
- Galvanized pipe 300 mm long to seat hotplate pole neatly
- Pole, grill and hotplate plus hook and billycan
- 50 mm galvanized pipe for drainage
- Timber formwork, pegs and nails for top collar slab

---

* Finished size: 1550 mm diameter and 350 mm deep.

The pit barbecue is bordered by an expanse of basketweave patterned paving so that people can gather around while the cooking is in progress.

2 Drive a peg into the centre of the pit area. Hammer a nail into the top of the peg with 20 mm protruding. Loop string around the nail, stretch it taut for 650 mm, loop it around a stick and scribe a circle on the soil.

3 Excavate the circle to a depth of 450 mm, keeping the sides vertical. With a club hammer drive 300 mm of galvanized pipe into the centre of the excavated hole. It should be slightly larger than the barbecue pole, which needs a firm but loose fit so that it can be withdrawn when not required. Check the fit before

concreting the base slab. Make sure the top of the pipe is exactly 100 mm above ground level, the same as the top of the concrete. This pipe can also provide drainage in sandy soils.

2 Drive a nail into the centre of the peg, and using string and a stick, scribe a circle onto the ground.

TOOLS

- Bricklaying tools (see page 15)
- Hacksaw for cutting galvanized pipe

---

4 Lay steel reinforcing mesh over a peg and use a taut string and permanent marking pen to scribe a circle with 600 mm radius on the mesh. Cut the circle with steel mesh cutters or an angle grinder. Position the mesh on mesh men in the base of the pit and make sure that it is clear of the centre pipe.

5 Concrete the base slab (see the section on concrete on pages 16–17), finishing the concrete just below the top of the pipe. Check pipe is vertical. Angle the slab slightly towards the sides where the drainage outlets will be. Allow to cure for 2–3 days.

BRICKWORK

6 Using a taut string and a coloured chinagraph pencil, scribe a 450 mm radius circle onto the base slab. Using this as a guide, lay out the first course of brickwork (see the section on bricklaying on pages 17–19). Insert

drainage pipe between the bricks, stopping at the scribed line. Excavate any necessary trenches and complete laying the pipe.

7 Mix the mortar and lay the bricks. Wide vertical joints will be created in the back of the circle, but they can be filled with mortar. Alternatively, you can cut all the bricks in half. Laying halves around a circle makes jointing easier. Lay four courses of bricks to complete the pit. Allow to dry.

8 Backfill to the top of three courses with a porous material such as aggregate or sand for good drainage.

THE SURROUND

9 Form up the surrounding square with timber formwork with its top 15 mm below the top of the bricks to ensure that run-off is away from the pit. Peg and nail the formwork into position and then check it is square by measuring the diagonals. If it is square the diagonals should be the same. Position four strips of steel mesh, 200 x 1450 mm, in the corners to give the slab strength.

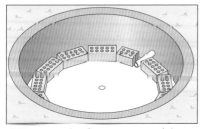

6 Lay out the first course and insert drainage pipes between the bricks, stopping at the scribed line.

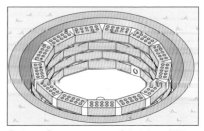

7 Lay four courses of bricks, filling the wide joints in the back of the circle with mortar.

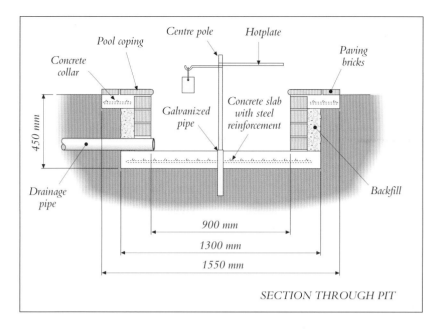

Centre pole
Hotplate
Pool coping
Paving bricks
Concrete collar
Galvanized pipe
Concrete slab with steel reinforcement
450 mm
Drainage pipe
Backfill
900 mm
1300 mm
1550 mm

SECTION THROUGH PIT

10 Pour the concrete so it is level with the top of the formwork. Finish the surface with a wood float.

11 Position the coping around the pit, adjusting the spacing to fit whole stones if possible. Scribe a line at the back of the coping as a laying guide. Remove the stones, mix mortar to provide a bed and lay them.

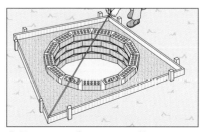

9 Form up the surrounding square with timber formwork and check for square by measuring the diagonals.

12 Set up string lines around the edge of the outside square. Spread a mortar bed and mortar the joints of the pavers as they are laid. Allow the coping and the pavers to dry.

13 To create the mosaic design in the corners, break up several paving bricks with a club hammer. Spread mortar in each corner. Position the pieces and tamp them down to the correct level with a straight edge held against the coping and the pavers. This ensures the correct slope.

14 After the mosaic pieces have set in the base mortar, grout the joints with a 6:1 sand:cement mortar mix. Sponge-clean the surface of the coping, pavers and mosaic pieces. Allow to dry.

Originally designed for wood firing with metal plates for the hotplate and base of the firebox, this barbecue has been converted to natural gas.

Stone barbecue

This brilliant barbecue with central hotplate is built from shaped sandstone blocks. The construction is not difficult, but cutting the stones to shape is very time-consuming.

DESIGN

Although the curved design of this structure requires careful stone-cutting, the operation of the actual barbecue is simple. The central hotplate has an area of 930 x 700 mm, originally heated by a wood fire. Both the hotplate and plate for the firebox base are removable. A functioning chimney opens into the firebox immediately below the hotplate. The walls and chimney, which is tapered to reflect the curve of the wall, are constructed of rock-faced sandstone blocks that have been hand-cut and faced.

MATERIALS★

- Concrete for slab: 0.8 m³ ready-mixed, *or* cement, sand and 10 mm aggregate
- A142M reinforcing mesh: 7 m
- Tie wire and mesh men
- Two 100 x 50 mm straight timbers 3600 mm and 2000 mm long
- Timber formwork with pegs and nails for slab
- Sixty sandstone blocks 500 x 200 x 140 mm
- Plywood for block template

- Chinagraph pencil
- Ten sandstone cappers 500 x 380 x 50 mm and two 800 x 300 x 50 mm
- Off-white cement, white bricklayers sand, lime and plasticizer for mortar
- Steel plate 800 x 400 x 10 mm
- Steel rod 200 x 8 mm diameter
- Non-silicone water seal to protect stone
- Two steel plates 930 x 700 x 12 mm
- Copper pipe or expansion bolts

★ Finished size: 3320 mm wide and 1675 mm deep; chimney is 1470 mm high.

The barbecue has two curved wings, which enclose a court with sandstone flagging laid in a stretcher pattern. The ends of the two wings and the two centre walls are faced with blocks to give a buttress finish. The tops of these wings and the curved walls are capped with overhanging slabs of sandstone.

SETTING OUT

1 Lay the 3600 mm length of timber on the ground for the front of the barbecue. Drive in pegs either side of it to fix it in position. Hammer a 100 mm nail into the exact centre of the timber, so that it projects 50 mm.

2 In the 2000 mm length of timber drill a 5 mm diameter hole, 100 mm from one end. Locate and mark two positions 1300 and 1700 mm from the drill hole. At each mark hammer a 100 mm nail through the timber.

3 Place the hole over the centre nail of the fixed length of timber and rotate the 2000 mm timber in a semicircle so that the protruding nails scratch lines in the ground to indicate the front and back of the footings respectively. Leave the fixed board in position.

4 Excavate 300 mm deep trenches for the footings: the 400 mm wide curved wall plus 300 x 1100 mm at the back for the chimney and 700 x

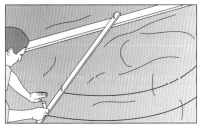

3 Place the hole over the nail in the fixed length of timber and rotate the shorter timber in a semicircle.

HINT

You may find it easier to have the curved stones precut by a professional stonemason, or they can be cut to your requirements at the quarry.

300 mm for each of the centre arms (see the diagram opposite). Lay the trench mesh. To bend the straight mesh around the curve, cut it in several places, kink it around the curve and retie it with tie wire. Fill the trenches with concrete and allow it to set for 2–3 days.

5 Take the nails out of the 2000 mm timber and mark two new locations at 1400 and 1600 mm from the drill hole. Once again, rotate the timber around the surface of the concrete, scribing two lines with a masonry pencil. Use these two curves as a guide when laying the blocks. Also mark guidelines for the centre walls and chimney. Adjust how far the curved arms project by moving the

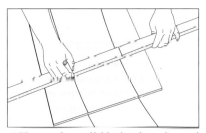

6 To cut the wall blocks, lay plywood on the footing and scribe the curved lines onto the plywood.

fixed timber in as desired (in the barbecue on page 56 the timber was moved in 150 mm for a courtyard depth of 1250 mm). Again fix it firmly in place and leave it at least until the end blocks have been laid.

CUTTING THE STONE

6 Cut all the blocks for the curved wall to shape before you begin laying (see the box above). Begin by making a template of the required shape. Lay a 600 x 400 mm piece of plywood on the concrete footing over the drawn lines. Rotate the timber to scribe the curved lines onto the plywood. Again using the rotating timber, mark the lines for the ends of the blocks square to the curve and 500 mm apart, so that a complete block shape is created. Cut out the shape with a jigsaw.

7 Prepare a good solid bench (there should be no bounce) at a height that will allow you to stand up straight with an undressed stone beneath the stone being cut. Ensure the surface and blocks are clear of dust and grit.

8 Place the template on top of a block of stone and mark the shape

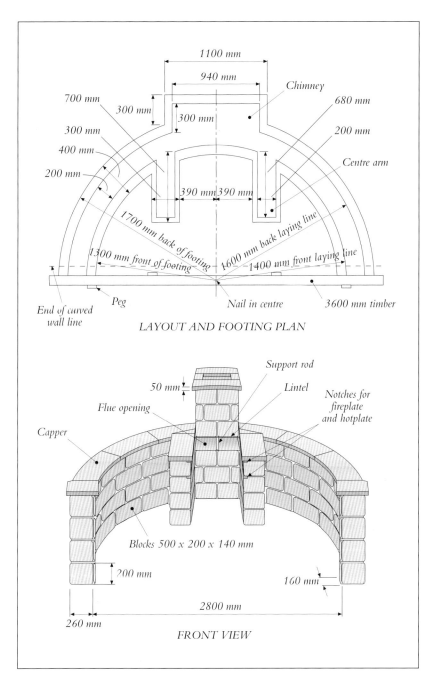

1100 mm

940 mm

Chimney

700 mm

300 mm

300 mm

680 mm

300 mm

200 mm

400 mm

200 mm

Centre arm

390 mm | 390 mm

1700 mm back of footing

1600 mm back laying line

1300 mm front of footing

1400 mm front laying line

Peg

Nail in centre

3600 mm timber

End of curved wall line

LAYOUT AND FOOTING PLAN

Support rod

50 mm

Lintel

Flue opening

Notches for fireplate and hotplate

Capper

Blocks 500 x 200 x 140 mm

200 mm

160 mm

2800 mm

260 mm

FRONT VIEW

with a coloured chinagraph pencil. Using a power wet saw with a 300 mm diamond-tipped blade, cut along the two end lines.

9 Square two lines from the marked curves down each cut end of the block. Turn the block over and place the template so it is in line with the vertical end lines before marking around the template again. Use a club hammer and bolster to cut the curved faces. Turn the block over regularly and work back gradually to the marked lines. Remove the sharp edges with the carborundum stone as you go. Cut sufficient blocks to complete the curved wall. It takes a professional stonemason 40–50 minutes to complete each stone, so don't be surprised if you have to spend an hour or more cutting each block. This work must be done carefully and cannot be hurried.

LAYING THE STONE

10 Mix the mortar using white sand, lime and off-white cement, matching the colour of the stone as closely as possible. Use a plasticizer if you want to make the mortar more pliable (see step 13 on page 18).

11 Start laying the first course at one end by putting a bed of mortar on the footing inside the marked curve. Lay the blocks to the centre of the curve, making sure they are vertical and level. Tap each into the correct position with the handle end of a club hammer, a rubber mallet or a block of 50 x 50 mm hardwood.

12 Lay from the other end to the centre. This means that any cut blocks in each course will occur in the centre, which will eventually be hidden by the firebox and chimney. Complete the first three courses.

13 Repeat for the fourth course, but leave out the centre two blocks to form the flue opening and to tie in the chimney. Using a circular saw with a masonry blade, cut a notch (25 x 25 mm) along the top edge of the third course of the flue opening. This notch will support the firebox plate and provide a seal to protect the stone from the smoke and soot.

8 Place the plywood template on top of a block of stone and mark the shape with a coloured china pencil.

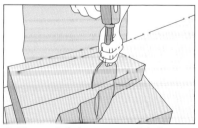

9 Use a club hammer and bolster to cut the curved faces, working gradually back to the lines.

THE CHIMNEY

14 Cut the blocks for the chimney in the same way as those for the curved wall. The chimney tapers 105 mm from vertical on each side when measured from the base to the top (see the diagram at right). To achieve this, the outside end of the end blocks for each course tapers 15 mm. Set a sliding bevel at the appropriate angle to taper 15 mm for every 200 mm of block height. Using the bevel, mark a cutting line. Cut the blocks for the chimney and then dry-stack them to make sure that you are happy with the fit and the taper.

15 When you are satisfied, mortar the blocks for four courses in position. The first three courses butt against the curved wall, and the fourth is tied into it with two blocks.

16 Use the block template to mark the shape on the steel lintel and take it to a workshop that does oxy-acetylene cutting. Position the lintel on the overlapping blocks to create a flue opening and support the upper courses of the chimney. The lintel should be recessed 50 mm so that a ledge is left to support the hotplate.

17 Lay the remaining three courses of the chimney.

TO FINISH

18 Using the remaining stone blocks, construct the two straight arms in the centre. Butt the first two

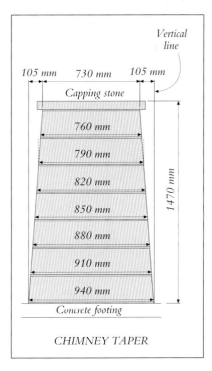

Vertical line

105 mm   730 mm   105 mm

Capping stone

760 mm

790 mm

820 mm

850 mm

880 mm

910 mm

940 mm

1470 mm

Concrete footing

CHIMNEY TAPER

courses against the curved wall. Before laying the third course, cut a 25 x 25 mm notch from the inside top edge of each block as described in step 13. Repeat for the fourth course to accommodate the hotplate, and then lay the fourth course.

19 Lay the sixteen face blocks on the ends of the curved walls and centre arms. Those in the third and fourth courses of the arms are notched (50 x 25 mm) for the fireplate and hotplate. The face blocks are simply butted on. If you want to key them into the wall, drill 13 mm holes, which are then plugged with a 12 mm copper water pipe, or you can drill holes at a

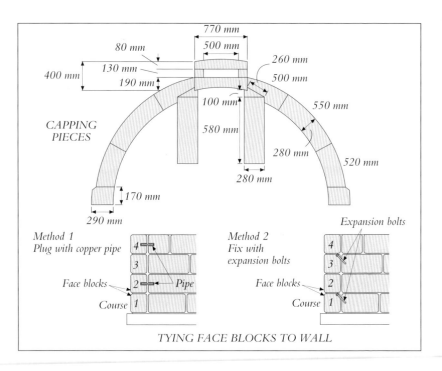

770 mm
500 mm
80 mm
130 mm
190 mm
400 mm
260 mm
500 mm
100 mm
550 mm

CAPPING
PIECES

580 mm

280 mm
280 mm
520 mm

170 mm
290 mm

Method 1
Plug with copper pipe

4
3
2 — Pipe
1

Face blocks

Course

Method 2
Fix with
expansion bolts

Expansion bolts

4
3
2
1

Face blocks

Course

TYING FACE BLOCKS TO WALL

45 degree angle and secure the blocks with 125 mm long expansion bolts. Place small timber wedges in the notched areas to prevent movement while the mortar is drying out.

20 Cut the capping pieces to cover the curved wall and centre arms. To

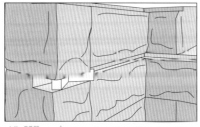

19 When laying the face blocks place wedges in the notched areas to prevent movement while the mortar is drying.

cut the curved pieces, make a template for the capping pieces as in step 6, but make the capping pieces 250 mm wide. The two chimney capping pieces are each cut from one solid piece of 800 x 300 mm stone, curved at front and back as for the curved wall blocks.

21 Because sandstone is porous, it is best to seal it before you use the barbecue in order to protect it from grease and smoke stains. Check the sealant manufacturer's directions and conditions of use before applying it.

22 Allow the mortar to set for at least two days, remove the wedges and insert the fireplate and hotplate.

Tools for building barbecues

Some of the most useful tools for building barbecues are shown below. Build up your tool kit gradually – most of the tools can be purchased from your local hardware store.

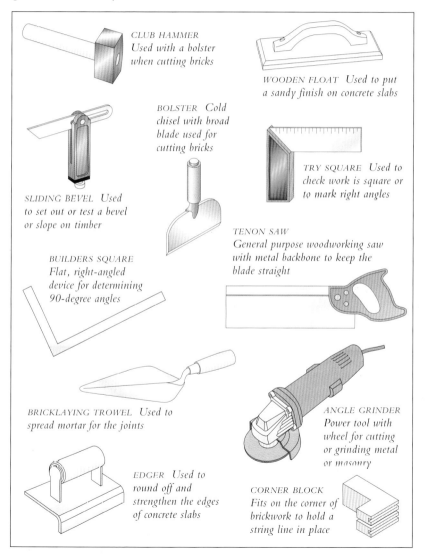

CLUB HAMMER *Used with a bolster when cutting bricks*

WOODEN FLOAT *Used to put a sandy finish on concrete slabs*

BOLSTER *Cold chisel with broad blade used for cutting bricks*

TRY SQUARE *Used to check work is square or to mark right angles*

SLIDING BEVEL *Used to set out or test a bevel or slope on timber*

BUILDERS SQUARE *Flat, right-angled device for determining 90-degree angles*

TENON SAW *General purpose woodworking saw with metal backbone to keep the blade straight*

BRICKLAYING TROWEL *Used to spread mortar for the joints*

ANGLE GRINDER *Power tool with wheel for cutting or grinding metal or masonry*

EDGER *Used to round off and strengthen the edges of concrete slabs*

CORNER BLOCK *Fits on the corner of brickwork to hold a string line in place*

Index